QUEENSGURL EST. 1960

QUEENSGURL EST. 1960

By JILL WILLIAMS

SELF-LOVE IS THE BEST LOVE

XULON PRESS

Xulon Press
2301 Lucien Way #415
Maitland, FL 32751
407.339.4217
www.xulonpress.com

Paperback ISBN-13: 978-1-66285-971-7
Ebook ISBN-13: 978-1-66285-972-4

Table of Contents

Dedication

This book is dedicated to God, the Most High, for continuing to love, protect, and guide me. I am humbled for this opportunity to share a small portion of my journey led by Spirit. To my children, grandchildren, and ancestors who came before me and who are always with me. Kayla, thank you for helping me realize how important it was to get this done. To my children, being chosen by God to bring you two into this world has been my greatest gift. I am very proud of the adults you have become. I have made my fair share of mistakes, but one thing I want you to always remember about your mother is that I am a survivor. My love and partner, EBW, thank you for always lifting me up and allowing me to be great, and for always having faith in me when I didn't have it for myself. Big brother, Cousin George L Williams, you have been holding me down from the sandbox to the present, and you are always a shoulder to lean on when I need one. Gina Renee Foster, words cannot express how I feel without you being here in the physical world, but I know you are here with me in spirit. Cousin Reginald Oliver, thank you taking the time to be a big brother to me when my older brother was not there. Stephanie Stokes-Oliver thank you for your professional input. Wesley Copeland, nephew, the keeper of secrets, thank you for always having my back. Jonathan Copeland, great-nephew, you were born for greatness. Keith Gordon-Oliver, my partner in crime from the cradle to the grave.

Much love to all my family, friends, and extended family members.

God bless you all!
Without God, I would be nothing.
As above, so below.

Introduction

$\mathcal{I}$ sat by my mother's bedside in silence as I watched her wither away from complications from the AIDS virus every day for months. I carried so much regret inside because there were so many things left unsaid between us. I practiced what I wanted to say to her over and over in my head, but when I would visit, I would just sit there and stare at her. One visit I will never forget, which stunned and frightened me at the same time. I was about to stand up, and my mother reached up and grabbed my arm with such force that it caught me completely off guard because she held on to my arm for dear life. I sat back down and assured her I'd be right back, but she did not utter a word. For many months as she languished in that hospice, I thought my mother could not talk. I thought the illness took away her voice because she never spoke to me. Years later, I found out the laugh was on me. One of my relatives was reminiscing about his visits with her and how often she made him laugh. I said, "Hold up, she could talk?"

He said, "Yes." They shared my laughs and conversations together. Which means she could speak all along. My mother chose not to speak to me, which was typical behavior for her but it did hurt my feelings.

All I could say was, "Ain't that a bitch." All that time, she only acted like that with me. Even toward the end of her life on earth, she found a way to slight me, and I could never figure out why.

You see, my mother was not easy to love, but I can only speak for myself because other people who loved her may not feel as I do. My relationship with my mom was always up and down, side to side, in and out, love and hate. I was convinced she hated me during her battle with this disease. One day, I had to take my children and get out of the house for a few hours of peace. We left the house, and the kids sprinted down the block. I got as far as the house next door and my mom came out on the porch and yelled to the top of her lungs, **"I WISH IT WAS YOU!"** That stopped me dead in my tracks. I turned around and looked at her, and she had so much hatred in her eyes. All I could do was hang my head and walk away. I could not believe what I just heard. That stayed and festered in my spirit for years. Some things just cannot be taken back. It was difficult for me to distinguish if she really meant it or if it was the disease running its course.

My mother was sixty-three years old when she was diagnosed HIV positive; this was in 1991. There was nowhere near as much information and medication available back then as there is now. People were afraid to be near anyone with HIV. I was ashamed and told people my mother had cancer. She already had many health issues that she was dealing with prior to the diagnosis. I also truly believe she was bipolar, and I know for sure she suffered from depression. Back in the day, we just did not know what to label it or even how to address mental health issues, especially in the Black community. You were just labelled as crazy.

My mother started to journal before her transition about her innermost feelings regarding contracting AIDS, her perception about her children, and her fears about being alone. Once I found it, I decided to keep the journal entries, as painful as they were to read. But since it was written by her, I felt keeping it was keeping a piece of my mother's spirit alive. Due to complications from AIDS, my mother developed dementia. I was able to discern how jumbled her thoughts were becoming and how rapid the disease was spreading by what was written.

First Entry, February 1992:

I don't have much money left, and I am too sick to work. I don't know how I am going to manage. I guess I will have to file for bankruptcy or try to put the house up for sale. I just need help, and I don't have any. The wasting syndrome has begun. I take lots of vitamins and try to walk a little for exercise. I don't know how long I'll be able to hang in there. Every activity that I have to do seems like I'm on the outside looking in. Sometimes it seems as though I'm invisible and no one can see me. When I go shopping for food and necessities, get prescriptions filled, put garbage out, and all of the mundane things that this dull existence calls for, it's as though no one sees me or even knows that I am in the world. I know that I am already dead completely because I have no life! I guess it's because I can't relate to the world or the people around me. It's like I can't wait to leave this foreign place. The children and adults are like aliens to me. You see, my only sibling, my brother, is in Arizona. All of my family is gone. The world that I was a part of has vanished. There is no one alive whom I can even talk about my past or a part of my past life with. If I'm lucky enough to sell my house, I won't have to worry about having enough money to live off until my death, which I feel won't be too long from now.

Oh, God! I pray, help me go as easy as possible! My beloved had cardiac arrest caused by AIDS. Sometimes I try to imagine that he is here with me, and I talk to him, and somehow, it seems to give me a little strength to get through the next day. I wonder how long will I be among the living? I just heard the news that a cure for AIDS will probably be discovered by the turn of the century or the year 2000. That's eight years from now. I don't think I will last two years more, but I am happy that something will stop this terrible thing. I'm afraid I didn't make a small dent in this old world.

I am so afraid now. Living alone like this is unbearable. I hope I don't take my own life. Things are not going well for me, either mentally or physically. I need help desperately, but I have no one to turn to. No one has time for me. That is, so called "family members." I've never felt so strange in my life. This virus is really rough. I'm constantly in pain, and I'm glad that I can manage to be alone for a while. Each day I feel lonelier and lonelier. Sometimes, it's like the floor suddenly fell out from under you and you start to fall into a bottomless pit. I guess it must be like slowly dying. I realize more and more that no one has ever loved me. I think I was just tolerated yet despised. Only James Sanders has ever loved me truly.

I've asked my son to not have a funeral at all. I would prefer to be cremated and finish! I've gone to lots of groups and agencies, but I haven't been able to find anyone that can relate to a senior citizen with AIDS. One dear friend that's in this world with me is my mental therapist. She has been with me since I discovered that I had been exposed to AIDS. She knows when my love died, and she knows when I tested positive six months after he was gone. She has been there for me for almost three years. It will be three years in June.

The only real thing I wish for is to be in a warm place where the sun shines every day, and I could enjoy looking at the beautiful flowers and enjoy being outside. Since I can't afford it, I must die in this dirty, filthy city of New York. I used to be a strong, proud person and a hard worker. Now, everything frightens me, and I am a nervous wreck. There are not many people who know this because there are not many people who see me. If only there was someone who showed a little concern for me, I think it would make my dying easier, but there is no one.

Second Entry: April 10, 1992

*W*ell, it has been a bad time for me thus far this month. On the sixth, I was told by my doctor that I have hepatitis of the liver. I have no idea as of yet of the outcome of this. My last T-4 cell count was 214. I'm told that at 200, I will have full blown AIDS. However, the fifth of this month was the anniversary of James's, my beloved's, death. So, I have been a little low. It's not so hard dealing with this death penalty but dealing with my everyday living and everything alone is becoming increasingly difficult as each day passes. It makes me miss my love more. Sometimes I wish we could have been sick together and been able to be there for each other. I'm sad because I realize that there is no one on earth who really cares about how I feel, and that's very sad. I've never felt that way until I was alone and sick, so it's very hard.

I never hear from my only living sibling since he's unable to communicate. I am going to make arrangements with the lawyer to have my body cremated. I would like to make everything as easy for whoever disposes of me as possible. I want no funeral service. I am going to try to get into this research program for women at Beth Israel in Manhattan. They test with new drugs and see how you do. I'm not satisfied with the medical service that I am receiving. Even my grandchildren no longer care about seeing me since I became ill. The house is falling down, but I am *unable to do anything about it. It needs a new stoop, a new apron, and the sidewalk and driveway fixed. I'm just not physically able to handle it. I do wish I knew how long I have. I wish I could go somewhere warm and friendly for a few days.*

I don't have much money left, and I am too sick to work. I don't know how I am going to manage. I guess I will have to file for bankruptcy or try to put the house up for sale. I just need help, and I don't have any.

Third Entry: November 1992

I haven't written anything in a long time. I was very sick for quite a while. I had surgery on my lymph node under my left arm. It was a horrible experience, and I was so terribly frightened because I didn't trust the doctors. In these months, they really socked it to me. One good thing has happened in my little sad life. I contacted a doctor who first treated me when I first tested positive. He was in a clinic at a hospital where they sent me for treatment. The doctor quit the job, and I didn't see him for almost two years. I was 175 pounds the last time I saw him at the hospital, and three months ago, when I saw him again, I weighed 140 pounds. I have what is called the "wasting syndrome." I am also deviled by the oral thrush in my mouth and the abscess in my mouth. I have been diagnosed as having HIV-AIDS and the wasting syndrome. I am very weak, but I feel that my doctor is going to do as much as he possibly can to keep me alive as long as he can. He is a Black man and a wonderful human being.

I am now sixty-five years old and so weak. I have one friend—a man I met in the grocery store. He is an elder in the church and a widower. He has been a good friend. At first, I wouldn't tell him about my sickness, but I felt that wasn't fair, so I told him. I was sure he was going to run like everyone else has, but he didn't. He calls occasionally and asks if I need anything from the store and sometimes, he visits me and has a cup of coffee with me. It makes my day go a little easier. He listens to my troubles, and once, he took me to his church so I could get prayed over and get a prayer card put in by the minister. Once, he took me to McDonald's for breakfast. It was nice having fun eating with someone.

I wish I had words to express the love I felt for my late husband he was a strange and silent man. I'm sure I have never loved another human being throughout my lifetime before him. The feelings that we both felt for each other were strange and unbelievable for both of us. We were constantly amazed by the intensity of things and simply could not understand why it seemed to get better and better each day. By the time we had been together for five years, it seemed like it had been a whole lifetime. Now I am alone again and have been for two years, yet I know it won't be for much longer, and I'm sure neither one of us will even be remembered by anyone who knew us and supposedly loved us. I only know that I am so happy that I enjoyed such a wonderful love during my lifetime. It made me young, as happiness usually does, and sometimes I felt beautiful because he always told me so. He always brought me flowers and beautiful cards and lovely gifts and called me every day to ask how I was feeling and again when he was on his way home. Thank you, God, for having let me experience the feeling of being totally loved before I die.

Fourth Entry: June 17, 1993

ell, I haven't written anything for a long time. Many terrible things have happened to me, too many to mention at this time. This caused great distress for me, which is the worst thing that should be inflicted upon me, but it seems that's all I've received from relatives and even the people connected with helping people like me. Everything was negative. I was told a few days ago by the lady at GMHC, who was supposed to be my case manager and someone I could confide in or receive some small type of help from, that she felt I would be better off at some other facility that had a few older people. I couldn't believe that she had already closed my case and didn't even notify me. Everyone knows that GMHC has more funds than any other AIDS group in NYC. I guess they have no further use for me. I can no longer travel, and I have great difficulty driving, writing, walking, or taking care of myself. The city finally provided me with a few hours of help. Instead of twelve hours a week, three days, and four hours care from a home health-aid attendant, they gave me twenty hours. I'm so alone, and most times, I feel like I can't wait to leave this life.

I don't have enough funds to pay my bills. I'm afraid I'll become homeless. I'm already penniless. No one seems to want to even know my condition or watch me die. My two children are my worst enemies. I had to become helpless to find this out. The only thing either of them cared for was asking me for money or getting it from me every chance they could.

I weigh 135 pounds. The wasting syndrome is upon me. The doctor says I have cataracts and need to get an operation so I can see better. To have found love before I died … Some people never do. My biggest fault was trying to love my family and share everything I had with them. I thought they felt the same way about me, but they don't. It's just that when I realized it, I had to be completely helpless, and that made matters worse. I live like a hermit—always alone and never being with anyone. I try to keep my doctor's appointments and my therapist appointments. Only strangers call me. The visiting nurse comes once a week, so I'm sure I don't have long. I wanted so desperately to see my great grandson, Jonathan Ray. I'm not able to travel to Boston to see him, and no one will bring him to see me. I don't ask anyone for anything. I just try to get through each day. I know it won't be long, but it's so sad to die knowing that none of your family ever loved you. It was what I could do for them.

Nothing could've been further from the truth, Mom.

Taking It Back To The Beginning

*I*f you are from my neighborhood in Jamaica, Queens, New York, when someone says they are going or just came from "across the bridge," you know exactly what they are referring to. That bridge is the Conduit, and that bridge separated both my homes when I was growing up, and lucky for me, my school was accessible from either side. I was born in Elmhurst General Hospital in Queens, New York in 1960. That's back when Queens was considered the suburbs. The part of Jamaica where I grew up was once the home of Jamaica Racetrack, which was closed in 1959 to become a housing development. That housing development is called Rochdale Village. I remember the good ole days of going outside in the summer and having to be home before the streetlights came on. Riding bikes up and down those hills in Rochdale, hanging out in Baisley Park, playing handball at Woodrow Wilson High School, as it was called back then; now it is August Martin High School. At Rochdale movie theater, the movie changed every Wednesday. My mom and I would go after school because I had a half a day every Wednesday (a great perk of attending a Catholic school), and she would love to be able to go see a movie when the theater was half empty.

I have many bittersweet memories of good times, which helped balance out the dark ones. Times when it was just us two: Mom working nights, me waking up to an empty house. I was told repeatedly not to put our business in the streets; what went on in our house stayed in our house. When I came home from school, mom was asleep. Dinner was on the stove, homework got done, and the kitchen was cleaned up. I stood on a chair and washed dishes like my mom taught me. I'd get ready for bed as she got ready for work. That was the routine. I remember feeling so grown up at six years old.

Back when there were no cell phones, the grapevine moved faster than the speed of light, or so it seemed. If someone saw me do something or be somewhere I wasn't supposed to be, my mom knew before I got home. Everyone in the neighborhood knew each other and watched out for each other. Any adult could and did chastise you. These were the days when children respected adults and the authority they wielded, the days before the crack epidemic hit Queens and all the other boroughs of New York City and changed my safe neighborhood from where you could leave bikes out overnight and your doors unlocked to residents having to install bars over their windows and security systems in their homes.

Middle class hard-working Black people lived in my neighborhood. My friends' parents either worked for Con-Edison, Ma Bell, the United States Postal Service, banks, or as police officers. They all had regular jobs—all except mine. My parents both tried "square" jobs (as my mom referred to them) and were drawn to the street life. Fast money came and went. The allure of the street hustle and making fast money lured them in, and they seemed trapped. Unless you make wise investments, that fast money slips right through your fingers. My parents' associates came by, selling everything from filet mignon to jewelry to whatever the latest fashion was. Every hustle you could imagine played itself out at our house.

Growing up in Jamaica, Queens in the 60s, where turmoil and change were prevalent, had little effect on me. What I saw on television compared to what was going on around me seemed like it was a million miles away. The Civil Rights movement was in full throttle, and I did not fully understand racism until it happened to me first-hand. I attended a Catholic elementary school from the first through the eighth grade. They would partner us up and make us hold hands to go across the street from the school yard to the church, and a white boy refused to hold my hand. He said he would not hold my hand because I was a nigger. I was not sure what a "nigger" was, but I did know it wasn't a good thing, and my feelings were hurt. I went home and told my mother, and of course, the shit hit the fan. I don't remember the outcome or if there was any apology because I was only six years old in the first grade.

My school was predominately Italian and Irish back then. The school became more diverse by the time I was in the third or fourth grade. We had a few white families that lived on our block, and my best friend was a white boy that lived next door. We were about the same age and had no idea about prejudice. All we wanted to do was play and have fun. Kids are taught bigotry and hatred at home sadly it was taught then and still is in the present. I remember as more Blacks moved in, white families moved out, which permanently changed the landscape of my neighborhood.

If Those Walls Could Talk
(160-05 134th Ave)

*T*his is the home my parents bought together where I lived off and on during my childhood. My earliest memory at that house is being a latch key kid at six years old (a latch key kid is a child left home alone by a parent or guardian usually due to their work schedule. It was not uncommon when I was growing up). My mother worked nights at the post office. Nowadays, child protective services would've been called, but she was just doing what she had to do. My mother would lay out my uniform, and my cereal bowl would be on the table. I followed her morning instructions to wash up, get dressed, eat my cereal, lock the door, and dash down two blocks to catch the school bus. God forbid if I missed the bus. I did once, and I was out there crying, having a meltdown, when the mailman stopped and gave me a lift to school. As luck would have it, a friend of my mother saw me sitting in the mail truck when we stopped at a light. Of course, she snitched to my mom, and I remember how sorry I felt for the mailman more so than for what was in store for me. I need to be clear about Mom's character. Patricia Antoinette was not your typical PTA mom. Not by a longshot. My mother was "gangsta" before we knew what "gangsta" was. An "OG"(Original Ganger) is how she would be referred to these days by the younger folks.

My mother told me that working at the post office and as a toll collector on the New York State Thruway were the only "square" jobs she ever had. By the time I was in the third or fourth grade, my mom started working in bars as a barmaid. I was left home alone while I slept during the night. Sometimes after her shift, she did not come home when the bar closed. I remember hearing about an afterhours spot she frequented so much that I thought the owner was a celebrity. During this time, my father was in prison. I know he went in when I was about two years old and came home when I was around seven. He served five years, and my mother served one year in prison. I have a very vivid memory of the day he came home. My brother and I had been out, and we pulled up in front of the house as my dad was walking up the driveway with a brown paper bag in his hands. My brother was beaming because he adored my dad.

As I was walking towards him, we stared at each other while my brother was standing there grinning. Then he said to me, "Do you know who this is?" Then the recognition hit me. I screamed and jumped into his arms, yelling, "Daddy!" and he scooped me up, hugged me, and swung me around.

My mother blamed him for her arrest. I never heard anything good about him from my mother. I happen to look very much like him, so all I ever heard from her was how much I was like him and how I "wasn't going to be shit," like him. There was so much hushed talk back then. Back in those days, adults did not discuss those types of things with children. I never found out why they went to prison. When they were arrested, one of my aunts took me in, and I would be back and forth between her home and my mother's house. I kept a suitcase packed under my bed in each home during my childhood because that's just the way it was. When I turned fourteen, I decided not to go back to live with my aunt, and a year later, my aunt passed away, and that changed everything for me. Another huge regret I carried around for years was not saying thank you to my aunt for all she had done for me before she passed.

When I was growing up in that house, my dad stayed there off and on. Basically, he was on probation and needed an address and a place to lay his head. This was the only reason he stayed there, in my opinion. It damn sure wasn't because he wanted to spend time with me. It was such a strange dynamic to live in the same home with my dad without any interaction between us. As far as I was concerned, my uncle was my dad. He was the one who taught me how to ride a bike and disciplined me. I became detached emotionally from my dad to hide my hurt and anger for feeling like I was not a priority in his life and that I did not matter. As I look back, I realize that experience was laying the blueprint for my future relationships with the men in my life. I never knew exactly why either of my parents went to prison, but that is how I came to have two homes.

Mom's house and my aunt's house were total opposites. If the walls could talk at 160-05, they would have some stories to tell. My mom rented out our basement and sometimes my room when money was tight. There were times when the electricity and the heat were turned off. My mom always made it seem like a fun adventure when we had to use candles and flashlights or leave the oven door open for heat when the boiler would go out. I think I was the only kid that young who could check the boiler and knew what she was doing. The characters that came and went taught me so much about life, such as the original RuPaul who rented out my room. He was a female impersonator, and he would be flashy and glamorous, wearing wigs, gowns, make-up, heels, the whole shebang, on his way to work at night. Then when I would get up in the morning to go to school, I saw this little skinny average guy. My mom was such a character; she would get angry at him when he would get in his depressed mode and lay around crying, listening to his Billie Holiday records, then she would tell him to "put on some damn overalls and stop all that damn crying and be a man." She kicked him out after I got up one morning and I had to go in my bedroom for something and when I came out, she asked me if he was awake. I told her no, he was not, but his friend was. He broke the most important ground rule, which was not to bring any men home. All my mom heard was "friend" before she kicked in the door, snatched them both out of bed, grabbed her gun, and threatened both within an inch of their lives. The fur flew that day. Yeah, good times!

Then there was the couple straight from "down south" that lived in the basement for about a year. The wife was such a nice lady. I remember her babysitting me on many occasions. Her husband would get drunk every Friday and spend all the money, and they fought. He was the kind of drunk that always started fights but would get his ass whooped because he couldn't fight. His wife finally got fed up with him and moved out. He was the first person I ever saw my mother get physical with. Shit was hilarious. I can laugh now, but as a kid, I was petrified.

He owed my mom rent money and kept ducking her. I will never forget this as long as I live. One morning, we were both sitting in the kitchen. My mom was sitting at the head of the table, reading the newspaper, and never takes the paper from in front of her face. She is facing the door and was sitting close to the basement door. I was sitting at the table eating my break-fast. He knocked on the door, and when he opened the door, and while still reading the paper, she said, "You got my money?" Before he could say anything, she kicked him so hard in his chest and kicked the door closed in one fell swoop. All I heard was his ass hitting every step that led to the basement yelling all the way down, "Oh lawd, help me lawd!" My spoon stopped in mid-air. Remember, she never took the newspaper from in front of her face, then she peeked around, looked at me, and said calmly, "Finish eating, baby. It's all right." In my mind, I'm like, *NO! It's not alright! You just drop kicked a grown man down an entire flight of stairs!* Best believe he came with that rent and was never late again. Two things you did not do was mess with my mom's money or her family.

Then we had the lesbian couple who lived in the basement, Miss T and Miss J. Miss T was a nurse, and I thought she was so cool because she had a goatee and a mustache. They were very sweet and kind, and they both doted on me. They did their fair share of babysitting, and again, it did not seem out of the ordi-nary. My mom took in many people that had a difficult time fitting into society back then. Many people that came and went in and out of the house back then seemed like misfits out in the world, but to us, they were just regular people.

I remember my dad teaching me how to count money. He would dump money into the living room floor and have me stack the ones, fives, tens, twenties, fifties, and hundreds. One summer, I remember him pulling up to the house in a van with another guy, and they ran in with a rack of furs, which started a huge fight with my mom. I can remember a huge safe in our basement. Most of the arguments between them started when my mom tried to talk him into opening a legitimate business. It usually ended with him leaving for a couple of days.

There was also an ample amount of drugs laying around. My mom never hid anything from me. If she felt like smoking a joint or doing a line of coke, she did it. I thought everyone's mom had a small round mirror they kept on their dresser with a razor blade with white powder on it. I remember being curious and snorting it when I was ten for the first time. My nose starting bleeding and scared me half to death. My mom did not want to believe I was smoking weed at ten, so she sent me to spend the summer with my big brother. I did not know at the time that I was under surveillance, but when I was ten, I acted like I was sixteen, or so I thought. My brother was a jazz musician. When his buddies came over, out came the weed, so I would chime in and talk about the best kind of rolling papers to use and other things I thought were useful. He reported back to our mom saying, "Yep, she smokes because she knows way too much about weed for a ten-year-old." I will never forget the first time a joint fell out of my pocket in front of her. I was about fourteen or fifteen. I know she saw it, but she never said anything. To me, I thought it was because she did not care. It came up years later, and I asked her why she never said anything. She said, "How could I? You probably got it from me."

Across the Bridge
(145-24 176th Street)

$\mathcal{M}$y father comes from a large family. He was one of ten. There were eight girls and two boys. One of my aunts took me in; I am living proof that it truly did take a village. Back then, it was commonplace to live with extended family members. There were my three aunts, my grandmother, my uncle, and my cousin. I did not realize it until I became an adult and had children of my own that growing up in that household provided me with structure and laid a foundation that I will never forget. My aunt and her husband were the homeowners.

My grandmother lived there until her death when I was nine. Another aunt, my cousin, and a close family friend all lived there. I shared a room with the family friend, who we called aunt. My cousin had his own room across the hall. My cousin was, and still is, more like my big brother. My aunts were old school. They did not work outside the home, and they did not even drive. My uncle drove them everywhere they wanted to go. They cooked, cleaned, and took care of us. The daily routine when we got in from school was to change out of our uniforms, put on our "street" clothes, and do homework, then we were allowed to go out and play.

While we were outside playing, the aunts prepared dinner and set the table. They used real dishes; paper plates were unheard of. We did not eat dinner until my uncle walked in the door. You could set your watch by him. Once he came in, we knew the drill. Wash up for dinner, then we all sat down and ate together as a family every day. My cousin and I did what kids do: fed the dog under the table, kicked each other until being reprimanded; back then, all it took was the "look." Whether I was with the aunts, my mom, or any adult for that matter, you knew to check your behavior when they gave you the "look." I don't recall ever having to do chores other than make my bed daily. The aunts did everything for us.

When my mother was released from prison, I was about three years old. She had to rent out her home, so she came to live with us. There was constant friction between her and my aunts. The aunts were very much into church and religion, and my mom wasn't. My mom always complained about how they thought they were better than her. It was always drama. I was calling my aunt "mom" when she moved in, and my mom flipped. I can remember my mom telling me repeatedly, "I am your mommy. That is your aunt." She had to get a "square" job, as she called it, while on probation. I remember she worked as a cook in a group home for teens, and she would take me to work with her every day. When she finally was able to move back into her home, she took me with her.

Never A Priority

My cousin and I had a secret hiding place in the basement. I would go in there and sit and sulk sometimes. One time, I was downstairs in my hiding spot, which was an opening behind the bar that connected to the laundry room. When my dad came downstairs, I would watch him shoot drugs, which is known as "skin popping." I never said a word, I just peeked and watched. He never changed his demeanor. If I had not seen it with my own eyes, I never would have believed it.

My dad married when I was seventeen and had a daughter and a son. He had another family and life went on. He was a career criminal. He was in and out of jail for most of my life. I would sometimes see him and his other kids in passing, or I would ride my bike across town to the pool hall to find him, just to lay eyes on him. The last time I saw him, I was sixteen, and we ran into each other on the street. We were walking toward each other, and as soon as he reached me, he went in his pocket to hand me money. I told him I did not want or need his money and for him to go fuck himself. I was very angry and hurt, so I lashed out. Yes, another regret.

Unfortunately, that would be the last time I ever saw him. When my oldest child was born, I tried to find him, but then I received a letter from one of my aunts telling me he died, and she did not have any additional details. Many years later, a close family friend was visiting my mom at my mother's house, who happened to work for the New York State Department of Corrections, she asked me what my father's full name was. After I told her, she said she just processed his paperwork. He had gotten arrested and was ill and died while in custody. They transferred him to Elmhurst General hospital where he passed on. Ironically, that was the same hospital where I was born. Months later, I received an envelope with his police record from that arrest. It contained all the information pertaining to the arrest. I could see how sick and haggard he looked. I should have kept those pictures, but I burned them one night while in my feelings. I always felt like he did not love me and often wondered why. It took me many years to be able to confront my daddy issues and move on. I finally forgave him and I pray his soul is at peace!

I was so angry for so long at my father for not protecting me. As I mentioned, he lived in the same house and rarely interacted with me. I had conflicting emotions because my uncle was a pedophile. **Yes, I finally said it!** Sex never happened, but he was the "come sit on my lap" and constantly feeling you up type. Always near the bathroom when I came out from bathing—that type of shit. After I got older, I realized the aunts had to have known, but no one said or did anything. He was always trusted around kids, which was so crazy. He was the director of the youth choir, always picking up and dropping kids off, and the deacon of the church. Everyone in the neighborhood and church community loved him. He was well respected—hell, I loved him. When he grabbed his car keys, I was right there in his footsteps. Thus, the conflict.

When I was ten, I got my period. I was outside jumping rope, and it was summertime. I had white shorts on, and I will never forget it. After all the oohing and aahing from the kids, I went inside and into the bathroom, and I damn near fainted when I saw red. I laid out in the living room floor and told my aunts I was dying. No one made a fuss, but no one explained anything either. My aunt said, "Girl, you are not dying. Get up and go take a shower." She sent my cousin to the store for that huge purple box that said KOTEX on it and a crazy belt that was worn around your waist back in the day to hold the pad in place. Years later, my mom said she got the call from my aunt saying I had gotten my period and jumped in the car and drove over to see me, thinking I'd be laid up in bed. But when she got to the neighborhood, she saw me riding my bike with my friends, and she turned around and came back home after seeing I was alright.

The only time I remember anyone talking about anything sexual with me was my uncle. I had on my first training bra. I was nine (I developed early) and was in a hurry to get back outside to play, and he stopped me on the way out as I walked by. He said he heard I had a new training bra and asked if he could see it. So, I pulled up my shirt, and he felt my little nubs and said, "See what I am doing? Don't ever let boys do that."

I said "Okay," in a very matter of fact way and kept it moving. I never told my mother. I never told her many things' adults did or said to me that were hurtful because of my fear that she'd end up back in prison due to her temper. The first person I ever mentioned him to was with an older cousin, who was very honest with me and said he chased her around the house when she was fourteen and told me to talk to other female cousins. I was shocked at how he could get away with that for so many years unchecked. I could never wrap my mind around that, yet in all other ways, his character was never taken into question. Like I mentioned, he was well respected in the neighborhood. A family man, a great provider, but he was sick in his mind when it came to his sexual desires.

My uncle had this loud, distinctive whistle that he would do no matter where we were in the neighborhood. When you heard that sound, you made sure you jumped on that bike, skates, ran, whatever you had to do to get back home pronto. If we weren't on the block and our friends heard it, word would get back to us to get home. Amazing, with no technology like we have now, how fast word spread. How did we ever survive the 60s and 70s? I would not trade growing up in that era for anything in the world. There was change going on in the world, but things were always the same and constant for me living in that household.

I remember being at his funeral, and someone asked me if I wanted to speak. Hell to the no, because no telling what would've come out of my mouth. I recently found out he finally caught a case for his deviant behavior. He remarried, and the new wife's granddaughter said he fondled her, and they pressed charges on his ass. About damn time someone stepped up. I believe a settlement was agreed upon. The last time I saw him before he died, my cousin begged me to meet him at the house. I decided to bring my children because he had never met them. I think my children may have been around seven and eight years old at that time. I remember us sitting on that couch with plastic cushions, feeling ill at ease. The new wife had changed everything, so I felt very awkward and uncomfortable. You would've never thought I grew up there by how uptight I felt. My cousin sensed my discomfort and told the kids to come with him so he could show them my old room and the rest of the house. Once they left, my uncle said to me, "Why is this the first time I am meeting your kids?"

My response was plain and simple. "You know why." I couldn't wait for that visit to be over.

MISS NITE LIFE

A MIXOLOGIST, TOO—YET! Decorating the bar at Jamaica's Copa City is pretty Pat Copeland. She's calling attention to fact the Long Island nitery has started new policy of "live" music 6 spot six nights a week. When not posing atop bar, Miss Copeand dispenses drinks at the club.

*M*y mother, Patricia Antoinette Oliver, was the youngest of four children, born in Memphis, Tennessee in 1929. My mom carried so much bitterness in her heart from her early childhood in Memphis. She experienced racism firsthand. A white man spat in her face when she was seven years old for no reason as she was leaving a store, and older black men were outside the store and told her to go on home because they knew there was nothing they could do about it. She always talked about how bad her luck was to have been born during the depression. She had a strong hatred for white

29

people because of the injustices she witnessed first-hand when she was a child. It hardened her heart in a very profound way.

I don't know who she disliked more, white, or black people, because she used to tell me how cruel other black children treated her because of her skin color. In her very colorful way of talking, she always said if it wasn't for her mother, she was almost NOT born a nigga because her father's mother was Native American, and his father was white—as if that would have given her a better life. Who's to say? Maybe it would've. My grandfather was a brick mason. He was away from his family for months at a time, either trying to find work or working. My grandmother was a teacher and left Memphis when my mother was fourteen and found work in Manhasset, New York as a live-in domestic. (Fancy term for a maid)

My mom was a real beauty and had no fear of anyone or anything, was quick to fight, and had a reputation in the streets not to be messed with. I never understood how someone so pretty could be so gangster. Or was it just a facade? Many people only knew one side of her. The tough, street-wise beauty that could switch her personality in a New York minute depending on the circumstances. The woman who seemed fearless and strong to people on the outside looking in had no clue how weak and submissive she was when it came to the men in her life. Unfortunately, she looked for love in all the wrong places.

During my grade school years, I was back and forth frequently between Mom's house and the aunts' house. My mother always seemed to be embroiled in some type of controversy. There were the boyfriends some who beat her ass from time to time, which always resulted in me making a mad dash down the street, two blocks away in pajamas at one or two in the morning, knocking on our relative's door that lived down the block. (I never thanked him for being there for me in those days; another regret). I never understood how she was so tough on the streets but tolerated getting her ass kicked by these men. Not all men she dated were violent, but most of them were. In my opinion, once is too many when you have a young daughter at home witnessing this madness. So, it was constant arguments with my mom and my aunts, who felt she was not fit to raise me because every time it happened, I had to go back across the bridge for a few months.

My mother had a fear of being alone. As far as I can remember, there has always been a man in her life. Many of them resulted in disaster. She remarried when I was ten. That was doomed from the start and ended very tragically. The best thing that happened for me during that time is he had two daughters, one and two years older than me, and I was elated to have two sisters. I consider them my sisters to this day and always will. When I finally came back home for good, my mom was suffering from severe depression. She had gained lots of weight, and she slept all day. We reversed roles. I became the parent; she became the child. She taught me how to write checks and pay the bills. I became an expert at forging her signature, especially when it came to letters from school. I cooked, cleaned, paid the bills, and came and went as I pleased when I was fourteen. It took months for her to snap out of it and get back to being herself. For me, it was bliss. When she did snap out of it, she got a job as a toll collector on the New York State Thruway and worked nights. Our house was the party house. As soon as she pulled out of the driveway, kids were coming in the back door. I had the best weed because we were smoking hers. Of course, all good things come to an end. She double-backed one day and we were busted. Kids were running out the front and back doors like a cattle stampede.

Is it really a good thing to have loved and lost than not to have loved at all?

The Musician

My mother met Ray her first husband when she was a chorus line dancer, and he was a jazz trumpet player in New York City. They were nineteen and twenty years old, respectively. This is the mid-1940s, way before I came to be. Ray and Pat married and had six sons; the only one that survived infancy was my brother Keith. I often wondered what life would've been like had all my brothers survived. The life Pat lived as a young mother and wife with Ray, the musician, was nowhere near the life I would be born into. Uncle Ray, as I fondly called him, was always around when I was growing up. Even though divorced, they always remained friends and had a certain connection between them that was something only they understood. My mother was never able to heal the pain from losing all those babies. She had wanted a big family with Ray. She had a rare blood type; the RH negative factor or "blue babies," as they were called back then. They all lived maybe two, three months, then passed. All her children, including myself, had to have blood transfusions as soon as we arrived. I remember how she always remembered their birthdays. It would be an ordinary day, and she would say, "Kerri would be twenty-eight," or "Kim would be twenty-nine today," and that would be the end of the conversation.

She would tell me this story many times during my childhood. She said after the last baby died, she started talking to dolls, and with her incredible wit, she said, "I did a stint in Creed,"(her stint was a year in the psychiatric ward) referring to Creedmoor Hospital in New York City. She said every day for a year, Uncle Ray would bring Keith to see her; not bring him in, because he was very young, but bring him by her window so she could wave to him. I never knew if this really happened. I say that because my mom had at least ten different personalities and knew how to manipulate people and situations to suit her needs at any time. She was the most complicated person I have ever known.

When you are a child, you just think certain things are normal because that is all you've ever been exposed to. My mother always blamed her marriage failing due to her meddling mother-in-law. I always felt sad for my brother because he was always caught in the middle of a never-ending feud between our mom and his grandmother for his affections. He was always trying to be the peacekeeper between the two women in his life who loved him the most. He was fourteen years older than me. I cannot remember him ever living with me and our mother. He lived with his grandparents and stayed with his dad, who lived nearby. The constant bickering between our mom and his grandmother took a toll on him. When my brother told me stories about our mother when he was younger, it was difficult for me to wrap my mind around the fact that he was talking about the same person. It was a different space and time. Ray, Keith's father, was a jazz musician back in the 40s, and my mother was a dancer. I try to imagine what life must've been like for her during that time. She suffered an injury once while dancing and injured her back, and she was never able to dance again. My mother never mentioned anything about her marriage to me or why it ended, but when they both passed, my brother and I were going through their paperwork, and we found three sets of marriage licenses and three sets of divorce papers. No one can say they did not try to make it work.

The Hustler

That would be my dad. How he and my mother met or where they met was never clear. She told me she was a barmaid at a bar in Brooklyn during that time and that's where they met. I do not remember my mom ever saying anything positive about my father. He was to blame for everything bad that ever happened in her life, and for years, she would never let it go. An old school saying that many black families said back then was Mama's baby daddy's maybe (which questioned the paternity of a child) because my dad did not have any children until he was in his forties, and his sisters (there were seven of them at the time) did not think he could reproduce until I showed up. I do not remember my parents being together very long. I *do* remember constant fighting, and he would leave for days at a time. He was a quiet man and very well-liked by everyone who knew him. One weird situation occurred on the job. I was a corrections officer for the state of New York in the early 80s. One day, an inmate, who was a trustee and had been in for so long that he was no longer considered a threat, comes up to me and whispers, "You haven't changed in years." I asked him what the hell was he talking about. He asked me if I went to a Catholic school and said he shared a cell with my dad at a federal prison, and he stared at my picture every day for five years. I had to stay in CO mode, so I told him to get the hell away from me before I wrote him up. The irony!

The Barber

ᓚ

When my parents broke up, my mom's new love moved in. He was a barber by trade. I remember he treated us well at first. He cooked, cleaned, dropped me off and picked me up from daycare. I came across some old video footage recently of him grilling at a family cookout. Both him and my dad are in the video chatting it up and hugged each other. The Barber was very jealous when it came to my mother. My mom was a very beautiful women and was always the center of attention. I can remember hiding from him when he would pick me up from kindergarten. I could hear him yelling my name loud in the hallway. Even at a young age, I was embarrassed because he was loud and ignorant. One night, my mom and I had been to see a movie and came in late. I remember all the lights being out in the house, and when she put the key in the door and it opened, he hit her in the head with a baseball bat, yelling and cursing, saying she was out cheating on him. I took off down the street to our family member's house. I was pounding hard on the door. I had never been so frightened in my life. She had to get several stitches in her head. I always brushed her hair, and she showed me the stitches and made me touch it, which creeped me completley out. She stayed with him for several years. I could never understand how a woman who was so tough on the street and who had a reputation as someone who did not take any shit from anyone could take so much shit from the men in her life.

The abusive behavior went on until my mom was sick and tired. But during the years she was with him, the same routine happened often. She would call my aunt, and my uncle always showed up to pick me up to take me back to the house where I could find peace and stability for a little while. So be it if I had to be groped from time to time.

On and Off the Wagon

When I was ten, my mom remarried. He was a handsome, smooth operator. It seemed like they had only known each other for a couple of weeks before they dashed off and got married. What she did not know was that he was a raging alcoholic and had been on the wagon for quite a while. He did not mention that he was an alcoholic until after they wed. Once he took one drink, it was a wrap. He was a totally different person.

This relationship was full of drama. He tried to molest me as well as other young women in his own family. I did not find this out until years later. He was abusive and as mean as a snake and sexually aggressive when he was drunk.

There was one time we had a cookout, and I ran in the house to use the bathroom. When I came out, he called me in the bedroom and gave me a dollar. I said "Thanks" and put it in my pocket. In my ten-year-old mind, I was thinking about spending it when the ice cream truck came around later. He pulled me to him and rubbed my ass and whispered that he would have more for me if I let him in my room later that night. I was a nervous wreck after the encounter. I went into the kitchen and grabbed a butcher knife, which I stashed under my pillow. I went about the rest of the day, asking God to please not let him come into my room that night. Needless to say, of course he did. I remember he staggered into my room late during the night with his robe open, naked. I tried to fake like I was asleep, and he knelt down beside my bed. I lifted the pillow, so he saw the knife, and by the grace of God, he got up and left.

The next day, I didn't say a word to my mom except "I am going back to my aunt's house." I grabbed my suitcase and left. I did not come back to live in that house until I was fourteen.

Another abusive relationship. He beat my mom up when he was drunk, he went back on the wagon, returned to the nice, sweet, loving man she married, worked his way back into her good graces, then did the same shit over and over again until it came to a head. You reap what you sow is all I will say regarding that situation.

I'm Sure My Guardian Angels Drink Regularly

I left home when I was sixteen. I climbed out of my window, suitcase in hand, to avoid a pending beating. I had stayed out all night, which had become a regular pattern for me once I discovered a club in Greenwich Village called The Loft. I'd sneak out, take a bus and two trains to get there, meet up with my friends who were all grown, and dance all night. I'd stagger out early Sunday morning while the church folks were staring at me as I made my way home. I just did not care about any punishments. I was going to do what I wanted to do. By then, I had lost respect for my mom because of all the shit I had been through. I'm sure during that time, my mother was sick and tired of worrying about me hanging out, not knowing where I was or who I was with or what I was doing, and just fed up. She told my brother to make sure I didn't leave the house until she got there, and if I tried to leave, to whip my ass. He wanted no part of this unfolding drama. So, I decided I was leaving and no longer taking any more beatings.

I also thought I was in love. I went to the Bronx and moved into a raggedy walk-up tenement with my soon-to-be husband. I was sixteen, and he was twenty-one. I still went to school every day and managed to graduate. When I was nineteen, he decided to join the Marines and said, "In order for us to be together, let's get married."

I said "Sure," like it wasn't a big deal. We went downtown to the courthouse and got hitched; we didn't even have witnesses. He went outside and came back with a couple of tourists, who did not even speak English well, to be witnesses for us.

Over the next two years, we'd live in several different states and then I became a mother. I was twenty-one when my daughter was born on the Marine Corps Base Camp Lejeune. Eighteen months later, I gave birth to a son. We moved back home because he did not want to re-enlist. That's when the shit storm began. We lived in Harlem where he grew up, then in the Bronx. There was constant infidelity and domestic violence. We fought like Tyson and Spinks. I kept thinking of ways to end his life. My saving grace was always in the back of my mind: *If I go to jail, who is going to raise my kids?* Talk about history repeating itself. I'll never forget the day I finally left for good and went back to Queens to my mother's house. I strapped one baby on me and the other in the stroller and walked away.

That is my pattern. Leaving is what I've always done. Its what I do best!

I wore sunglasses all day to hide my black eye. After we put the kids down, my mother told me to take off the glasses, and I showed her my black eye and swollen face. During the time we lived there, it was constant beef between us. Just because she allowed me, and the kids to stay didn't mean she was happy about it. I always worked and took care of my children, paid my mother what I could, and was always consistent, but I had low paying jobs and was stuck in the cycle of poverty. I was among the working poor. Child support was non-existent, so I was on my own. I was in my twenties; a young mother of two with no direction, walking the tightrope of motherhood and being a party girl. Again, the cycle repeats itself. I was looking for love in all the wrong places.

That's why I know my guardian angel's drink. They meet at their favorite bar and swap stories about how exhausted they are from saving me from myself over the years. I almost came close to losing my life twice. A jilted lover pulled a gun on me. I laughed at his little .22 pistol, which enraged him. **Guardian angels to the rescue!** A crackhead tried to rob me and my date one summer night as we sat parked in front of my mother's house, chatting. He came up on the driver's side with his gun out and took my friend's ring, wallet, and keys. While they were arguing, I slipped out the car. I ran to the porch because I knew my mother always slept with her window open and heard the ruckus. Once I hit the porch, the door swung open, and she pulled me in. My friend told me when I was running toward the house, the guy pointed the gun to my back and my friend opened the car door abruptly to distract him so I could get inside. Fortunately my friend was unharmed and was able to find his car keys after the police arrived and helped us search up and the down the street until they were found. Again, thank you, angels.

My mother pulled a gun and a machete on me on a couple of occasions. **Guardian angels to the rescue.** Crazy times. Not until I had children of my own did, I fully know and understand how worrying about another human being feels. When I look back at my reckless behavior, it makes me shudder. It was the 80s; I was doing what everyone else around me was doing:

45

getting high and partying. My kid's alarm was set to 7:00 a.m. I'd be out all night, creep in at 6:55 a.m., get the kids up and ready for school, and have them at the bus stop, and I still went to work. I thought I was in control. My mother used to get high with me, so there was not much she could say. I felt she was a hypocrite when she tried to check my behavior. I knew she was fed up when one day, I came home from work, and she told me she'd call the authorities if I had a problem and have my kids taken away if I did not get my shit together. I knew she meant it; no more partying for me. All I did for the next year was go to work, come home, and be with my kids. I got down on my knees one night and prayed to God, asking for forgiveness and to not have my kids taken away from me. I had to surrender to a higher power. Prayers were answered.

Angels, thank you.

Fresh new start

In 1997, I moved to Alexandria, Virginia, starting a new chapter in my life and hoping for a better, brighter future for my children. I think it was the best decision I've ever made. It wasn't always rainbows and sunshine. I've stumbled along the way and had quite a few failed relationships along the way. I stumble and fall but always get back up, stronger than I was. I was thirty-six when I left New York. I am blessed to have sixty-one years under my belt. My children are grown and successful in their careers. I have three beautiful grandchildren that I love dearly. I've finally learned how to love myself unconditionally. There are many things I've done in my life that I am not proud of. I am now able to put the past behind me and move forward into the future. My journey wasn't always easy, but I learned from my mistakes, and I've stopped living my life full of regrets. I am a child of God, and I know I am divinely guided and protected by my ancestors, Holy Spirit, and angels.

"To Thine Own self be True" (William Shakespeare). William, thank you for that gem.

That is how I live my life now, being true to myself. Loving myself is the best love. Thank you, angels, for your guidance and protection. My angelic team and ancestors are always with me.

Forgiveness

My mother died from complications from AIDS in 1995. After all these years, I have finally found forgiveness, acceptance, and peace. I locked my feelings away and have been carrying around a heavy trunk of anger, shame, and low self-esteem for many years. I've finally come to a point in my life where I had let go of the past.

The most challenging experience in my life was being my mother's caretaker when she became ill due to completions caused by AIDS. She was not an intravenous drug user, but the man that she had spent the last eleven years of her life with was. He was a few years younger than my mother; he was the love of her life and vice versa. My mom had many unsuccessful relationships throughout my childhood, and I thought this one was no different, but it turned out to be the longest lasting, most fulfilling one she had ever had. I had never seen her so happy.

I came to love and admire him as well.

My children came to call him "Papa," and they developed a very close bond. He loved them, and they loved him. Everyone in my family loved him; he was a decent, honest, hard-working man during the week. But what we did not know was that on the weekends, he was sharing needles with his "other" friends. He had been able to keep that part of his life very separate from his "family life" for the entire five years that I lived there and even longer from my mother. My mom knew the street life and was a great judge of character. "How could she not know?" was my first reaction to the news.

He cleaned chimneys for a living; one day, we got a call saying he was on a scaffold nine stories high and the scaffold broke, and the only thing that happened to him was he shattered the bones in his right heel. Luck was certainly on his side that day. We rushed to the hospital to check on his condition, and later that night, he was released. My job was to take him to his weekly physical therapy sessions. After about three or four weeks, he ran a high fever and showed signs of what seemed to be the flu, but he just never recovered. We ended up taking him to the emergency room late one night, and he went from bad to worse. Tests were run, and that is how we found out he had AIDS. He was already in the last stage of the disease when we found out what was wrong with him; he was dead within a year.

After his death is when my challenge began. My mom was tested, it came back positive, and our lives were never the same. My older brother was offered a job teaching music in Germany. He was a jazz musician, a drummer; he took the job during this time, sat me down, and told me it would be my responsibility to take care of Mom because he was leaving the country. So, I did the best I could with what I had to try to protect my children and myself. I remember my mom telling me it was such a "lonely" disease. Being a senior with AIDS was also very challenging. My mother lived with HIV for five years; she found out at age sixty-three, and she made her transition at the age of sixty-eight.

I learned that life is precious and not to take the people you love for granted. I learned that people hurt the ones who are closest to them the most. I learned about the healing process; I am still learning and still healing. It takes TIME, and time is fluid. Healing for each person is different, putting the past behind you is not an easy task, and everyone has to deal with their pain in their own way. I learned what it means to mourn; it was something I did not get a chance to do after my mother's death because I was too busy taking care of everything and everyone. I learned that not taking care of myself and putting myself last was detrimental to my own health. I learned the true meaning of stress and that stress can kill you. I learned who my "true" friends were by who was there in my time of need. I learned not to take things at face value. I learned how to trust again. I learned how to let go of anger and resentment. Most of all, I learned the value of forgiveness.

If I could do anything differently, I would not be ashamed of anything. I would have interacted more with my children and realized I was not the only one who lost someone they loved. I would've been less selfish and not been so hard on myself. I would not have been so bitter and stubborn. My brother and I had a terrible argument and did not speak to each other for seven years after our mother's death. I would've communicated more with other family members. I would have held on to my faith in God that He would see me through, but instead, I was angry with God.

I have shared my story with others over the years who have found themselves in the position of being a caretaker. It is not easy, but it can be managed. People need to realize they are not alone and that they do not have to carry the burden all by themselves. You do not need to try to be superwoman or superman because you can't. Ask for help when you need to; you are entitled to a break. If there is more than one sibling, each should help share the responsibility and not place it squarely on the shoulders of just one. My message is directed to young people about HIV and AIDS prevention. Young people think they are invincible; they think "It can't happen to me," but I want them to know, if it can happen to a sixty-three-year-old grandmother, it can happen to you. AIDS does not discriminate. That is something we all need to understand in our society, that the choices we make in life can impact us for the rest of lives.

I did not have a choice in the matter. My brother left the country—it was up to me. I remember my brother calling a "family meeting." All my cousins showed up. All my mother's favorite nieces and nephews. Everyone told her "We are here for you, just let us know what you need, we will always be there." Once they walked out of that door, *no one* was there except me and my children. Phone calls are different from visits; people stayed away because they were afraid. Fear had a stronger hold on them than their love for her, so no I had no choice in the matter. I did what I had to do during those five years to show my mother I was a devoted daughter and that I loved her.

My mother was a force to be reckoned with. We always had a very strained relationship. My mother showed her love for me the only way she knew how. It took me many years to understand that and to try to understand her. Many people only knew one side of her. Despite our ups and downs, there was no one in this world that had my back like she did. She could cut you deeply with words, cuss you out for hours, but she always came through. There were so many things left unsaid between us before she left this realm that I have been carrying around in my heart for so long. Mom, I always loved you. I hope you forgave me as I have forgiven you.

End

Mom at eighteen years old.

Me, my big brother Keith and Mom

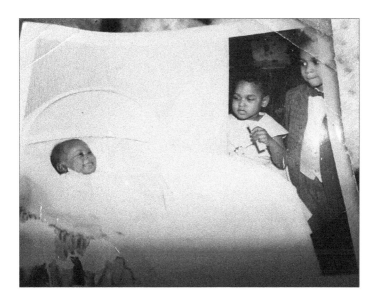

My cousin Gina looking at me like *"This kid is going to need my help."*

My beautiful grandchildren.

My brother Keith and son, Wesley, having a jam session.

Three generations of Copeland men.

Homage to my ancestors;
much respect, love, and admiration.

(QUEENSGURL)

CPSIA information can be obtained
at www.ICGtesting.com
Printed in the USA
BVHW021908271022
650482BV00009B/97